Black Friday 101

Tips & Tricks to Win the Day

R. L. Hudak

Dedication

This book is dedicated to the late Arlene (Vitale) Esley who stood in countless lines to ensure that I always had the hottest toy of the year and with whom I have very fond memories of later Black Fridays – sitting in the mall, playing our made-up 'Occupation Game.'
I miss you, Gram. Every minute.

.

Table of Contents

Get in the Game.

If you have decided to participate in Black Friday – I mean *really* participate in Black Friday – then plan to get in the game. Serious Black Friday shopping is not a last-minute decision. Plan early. Plan often. I personally train for Black Friday at various times throughout the year. This includes staying fit, keeping yourself informed, and yes, participating in a few shopping marathons.

To get the most out of this glorious day, I strongly recommend that you begin your Black Friday preparations shortly after the first of the year. Remember – this is not window shopping, nor is it a time to stock up on toilet paper and fruit snacks. This is serious, no-nonsense, deal grabbing. The following tips will help you to be better prepared than most of the shoppers you will encounter – and there *will* be encounters. So, let's get started...

Stay Ahead of the Competition.

If you do nothing else to prepare for Black Friday, do this. Subscribe to BFAds.net's mailing list. At BFAds, you can enter contests, buy t-shirts for the big day (a new design each year), and study buying guides for the year's hottest items. But most importantly, BFAds posts Black Friday ads as soon as, or even before, they are released to the general public. This goes a long way in planning for the big day. So, get one step ahead of the competition and check out BFAds.net today.

Accessorize Appropriately.

While you should most definitely have snacks, beverages, tissues, and wet wipes in a designated area in the car (backseat floor, passenger side), your purse or man bag should be of the cross-body variety only. Leave the grandma totes at home (not in the car – don't be careless). You must have both hands free at all times (when not grabbing bargains, of course). One of my teammates has a purse that is designated for Black Friday use only. It is small enough to stay out of her way, but large enough to hold all of the essentials. If you forgo the purse this season, be sure your pockets are large enough to hold your cell phone – this is an essential tool for the hunt. No pockets? Put cross-body purse at the top of your 'must-have' list this year. You can thank me later.

Speaking of accessories, don't miss this first opportunity to bust out your holiday gear (if you celebrate). My crew and I wear our annual Black Friday t-shirts from BFAds, but simple color-matching always works (though I'd avoid red and green). Matching outfits help to locate your teammates more easily, which saves time and gives you yet another advantage on the big day.

Be Alert.

Staying awake isn't good enough. Being alert, energetic, and constantly aware of your surroundings is what will set you apart from the competition. So, find what works for you and stock up, but remember – too much coffee = too many bathroom breaks = missed opportunities! That's why I opt for chocolate-covered espresso beans. Whatever your product of choice, it is critical to follow these guidelines:

1. Pack enough for yourself and your teammates for the big day.
2. Try out the product well in advance to ensure no adverse side effects (i.e. me + green tea = those missed opportunities we just talked about).
3. Take your metabolism into account when determining when you should have your first sip of coffee or piece of candy. There is no time to recover from a complete lack of energy in the midst of this event – plan ahead and stay energized!

Designate a Driver.

This is not because you will be consuming alcohol (see previous tip re: energy & alertness). A Designated Driver saves time in parking lots, keeps things moving in an orderly fashion, and prevents indecision during critical moments of the day. A good driver should be paired with an even better navigator, with the two front seats in the vehicle reserved exclusively for them. Here are a few sample questions for interviewing potential Black Friday drivers:

1. Do you own an SUV? If not, are you able and willing to operate one if it is provided for you?
2. Please rate your road rage on a scale from 'That's my parking space!' to 'My license suspension should expire in time for Black Friday.'
3. Are you now or have you ever driven professionally? (Bonus points for UPS, etc. drivers as they have the added skill of large package handling.)

Also, do not be afraid to request copies of license, registration, and driving record. Being pulled over or having to visit the police station will certainly throw off your schedule, so avoid that by screening your driver ahead of time.

Hydrate...But Not Too Much.

This is a physical activity, people. Keep the water and sports drinks on hand. But remember: too many bathroom breaks = missed opportunities! Plan your potty breaks ahead of time. Take turns pottying and waiting in the checkout line so that no second is wasted. And if you find yourself ahead of schedule (for more experienced shoppers), always use the time to hit the restroom, not the food court.

Suck It Up.

For most of my readers, Black Friday will be a chilly one. However, bundling up in your winter coat, mittens, scarf and hat is not the way to go. The stores will be H O T – and with every second a critical one, there will be no time for taking off those layers. Besides, where are you going to put them? Your hands should remain free at all times for grabbin' those deals! So, suck it up and leave your snowsuit in the car. Those 20 seconds from parking lot to store are not going to kill you. I typically run into the store, thus generating heat to keep me warm while minimizing travel time.

At the larger stores or malls, I recommend that the driver drop off the group at the door and then park the car. Just keep your cell phone handy so they can meet up with you later.

Don't Repeat the Past.

One of the things that makes Black Friday so exciting is that no matter how well we plan, unexpected things happen. A seasoned shopper will deal with these curveballs as best they can. But when hiccups occur, learn from them. Review the events of last year to ensure that you are prepared for those particular situations this year. For example, I no longer leave my aunt alone in Walmart. It's just too overwhelming for her (Read: Public Emotional Breakdown). There is no excuse for repeating past mistakes. New challenges will always arise – and from those you will make next year better.

Make a List. Check It Twice.

As you know by now, it is futile to go into Black Friday unprepared. To that end, a shopping list is a must. There are many ways to tackle this. Beginners may circle items in the ads and call it a day. But the serious Black Friday shopper knows that additional preparation is what sets them apart from the rest. I personally have a two-form system that has worked well over the years. The first is a master list that includes store names and hours (both regular and early bird). This will be used to formulate your final game plan and will also be an important tool for the navigator on the big day. The second form is attached to each store's ad. This is the shopping list for that store. Page numbers, prices, and sale hours (for those that differ by item, like Walmart) are all indicated on this cover sheet.

This can, of course, be done electronically. However, I've found that even though I work in the IT field, paper works best for me. It also makes for a great team building exercise. For the traditionalists, this would be done after Thanksgiving dinner. However, it is adaptable to any situation and team size.

Once each ad has a cover page, all team members gather together and circulate the ads. Teammates add their wish list items to the form (there is a column to indicate 'must have' items) and pass the ad along. Once this process is complete, the team leader (that's you), reviews all cover sheets and formulates the plan of attack (preferably while enjoying a piece of pie).

As you reach each store, grab only that store's ad with its cover sheet attached. It's quick, easy, and proven to be successful as I have never missed getting a 'must have' item since implementing this system in the early 2000s. (Read on to see how you can get these templates for free!)

For the techies, I will mention that BFAds has an app that allows you to view ad scans, click on items within the scan, and add them to an electronic shopping list. It also lists store hours, but these may vary by location, so check your local ads to confirm. Whatever method you choose, do not leave home without that list!

Practice Makes Perfect.

Training exercises are not just for athletes. One of the best ways to prepare for Black Friday is to practice throughout the year. I recently added simulations to my training routine, and I have seen great results. This is especially important for your less-seasoned teammates. In addition to the usual shopping marathons that should be staged throughout the year (going from store to store, pushing yourself to the limit, seeing just how long you can last), situational tests should be executed. These may include, no shopping carts at the store's entrance, no parking spaces near the store, emergency bathroom break, and companion has a meltdown. As you might have guessed, these are all situations that have happened to me in the past. I've learned from them, practiced how to respond, and now handle them with ease.

Don't Go Overboard.

Too much of a good thing is still too much. Do not train so hard that you are exhausted – or even worse, injured – for the big day. Think back to your school days. I did best on exams when I studied up until the night before the test then went to bed early that night. While grocery shopping on the day prior to Thanksgiving is an excellent training opportunity, it is just too close to Black Friday (even closer to those Thursday store openings). If you are not busy preparing for Thursday's meal, I recommend taking it easy on Wednesday night. Curl up with a good book (this one, perhaps?), a soothing beverage, and get to bed early. You won't regret it, especially when this extra bit of energy allows you to edge out your sleepy competition.

Quality Over Quantity.

Ok, I've avoided it so far, but here goes. Yes, yes, I know there is all this controversy about Thursday store openings. Honestly, the more people who boycott stores on this day, the better. That leaves the aisles clear and the sales aplenty for us hardcore shoppers. Whatever you choose, be aware that some stores hold sales on Thanksgiving Day that *differ* from their Black Friday sales. They do this for one reason: We show up! Whatever your feelings on Thanksgiving Day shopping (I scored a nice tablet one year at CVS while waiting for the turkey to cook), think quality over quantity.

A mistake that I've made in the past is to try to hit all of the big box stores regardless of their opening times. This had me starting at 8pm Thursday night and going through Friday mid-morning. For my younger readers, I say go for it! For the rest of us, my advice is to choose wisely. Plan for either a late night or an early morning, but not both. If possible, make the decision based on the deals. If you need a new TV, make that your priority. If the best TV deal is at a store that opens at 11pm on Thursday, build your schedule around that.

For me, Menards continues to have fantastic deals each and every year. Since this is my 'must hit' store and opens at 6am on Friday, I will build my schedule around that. I may hit a 6pm or 8pm store opening, but I will be in bed by 11pm in order to line up outside my golden store by 5:30am on Friday (any later and I won't snag a shopping cart, which is the key to success at this particular store – learned from experience on that one).

There is no right or wrong answer to this – just be smart about your planning to ensure that you do not run out of steam before you've gotten all of the 'must have' items on your list.

Forgive and Forget.

Emotions will be running high on Black Friday, and it will be very easy to get caught up in the anger, frustration, and disappointment that sometimes comes with this event. Rise above it all. Your teammates may be cranky and annoying. Remember, you are annoying them, too. Let it go and move on. There is no time for arguments today – and tomorrow when you're basking in the glory of your bargains, all will be forgotten.

Also, keep in mind that the store employees are mostly minimum wage workers just trying to get through the day. Don't take your anger out on them. And finally, should you encounter any pushing or shoving, ignore it and move on. The few seconds that it takes to turn around to see who just gave you an elbow to the head could very well be the difference between victory and missing out on the last $3.00 toaster. Stay tough. Stay focused.

Sharing is Caring.

I know that this tip does not seem to be in line with my theme but hear me out. I encourage you to read, prepare, train, and plan for the big day **with others**. Now, I am not talking about the lady next door who is out for the same $2.00 bath towels that you desperately need. However, I do recommend educating your family and friends on the proper way to have a successful Black Friday. Doing so can only make *your* Black Friday more rewarding.

Just think – the more soldiers you have on the ground, the more ground you can cover, increasing not only your chances of success but also the size of your overall haul. Yes, you can and should take credit for their purchases – you did the work, formulated the plan of attack, and led those soldiers to victory! So, share these tips (who wouldn't want this book as a gift instead of the usual socks or tie clip?), schedule and lead your own training and planning sessions, and let your little brother fight the crowd at Walmart while you hit a more low-key store in the meantime.

Get Excited!

Black Friday is tough, grueling, and long. But those veterans who have tasted sweet victory on this, the most glorious day of the year, know that most of all, Black Friday is exciting! So, follow my tips carefully, remember to breathe (use that morning breath to thin out the lines at the register), keep in mind the words of the great Vince Lombardi, "Winning isn't everything. It's the only thing," and most of all, GET EXCITED!

Bonus Tip 2017

You can find deals on everything from pencils to deodorant if you know where to look. The best places for these sales are drug stores. CVS and Walgreens, for example, not only offer great prices but have several rebate offers that equate to getting FREE products!

Worried that this isn't the best use of your time? Thinking that you need to focus on the big-ticket items? Well then, I've taught you well.

The real tip here is to hit these stores on Thanksgiving Day. Schedule a stop or two on your way to family dinner, or plan to sneak out while the gang is starting a fifth game of charades. These stores are open all day and will not be crowded, so you can be in and out in a flash...with a lot to show for it!

Bonus Tip 2018

So, you've mastered the basics and have even scored some free toothbrushes between the turkey and pumpkin pie. What could you possibly need to learn?

Oh, dear reader, we've only scratched the surface! Let's get a bit more advanced for this year's Bonus Tip...

As you now know, every second counts during Black Friday events. Are you spending those precious seconds in the checkout line? If you're shopping with a group, this 2-for-1 tip is for you!

First, be sure that your team is spread out among multiple checkout lines. Monitor the situation closely and know the signal (practice it ahead of time)! When the time is right, regroup into the fastest checkout line. Tricky? Yes. Impossible? Definitely not. It helps here if you have one cart for the group to share. If not, smile, be polite, and say to your teammate in your most innocent voice, "Oh, there you are!" as you squeeze your way to the front of the line. A dirty look here and there is a small price to pay for the time you will save with this tactic.

And for even more efficiency, complete only a single transaction during checkout. If you are trying to rack up those airline miles for your summer vacay, now is the perfect time to volunteer to pay for everyone's purchases using that airline credit card. You can settle up later when time is not of the essence. This is also the perfect time for those who missed the earlier tip about hydration to hit the restroom and for the designated driver to pull the car around to the front for loading or at least get those seat warmers cranked up to the highest setting.

Author's Notes

I do not work for, nor am I compensated by, BFAds.net. I am simply a fan citing this website with permission.

Vince Lombardi quoted from memory, but for citation purposes, please reference http://www.vincelombardi.com/quotes.html.

Have a tip or crazy-but-true Black Friday story? Share via an email to hudakauthor@gmail.com for a chance to be featured in a future edition!

Acknowledgements

A very special thank you to Valerie Piatak (aka A. Val) for not only her advice on this book, but for being my second in command during many Black Fridays past and future.

Thank you also to Omar A., Phil P. and Zahia R. for previewing this book and offering your invaluable feedback.

About the Author

R. L. Hudak, known as the 'Master of Black Friday' by friends and family, has successfully secured thousands of dollars in Black Friday savings during the past decade alone. R. L.'s Black Friday shopping experience began in the late 80's and spans multiple U.S. cities and states.

Follow R. L. on Facebook at https://www.facebook.com/hudakauthor/ .

Free Stuff!

For pdf files of the two templates mentioned in this book, send an email to hudakauthor@gmail.com or visit https://www.facebook.com/hudakauthor/ .

To view these files, download Adobe Acrobat Reader for free by visiting https://get.adobe.com/reader/ .

www.ingramcontent.com/pod-product-compliance
Lightning Source LLC
Chambersburg PA
CBHW070135290526
45789CB00005B/2256